T0209745

Simple Italian Cooking My Way

FRANCIS DICANDIO

authorHOUSE®

AuthorHouse™
1663 Liberty Drive
Bloomington, IN 47403
www.authorhouse.com
Phone: 1 (800) 839-8640

Published by AuthorHouse 08/26/2019

ISBN: 978-1-7283-2468-5 (sc)
ISBN: 978-1-7283-2466-1 (hc)
ISBN: 978-1-7283-2467-8 (e)

Library of Congress Control Number: 2019912814

Print information available on the last page.

Dedication

I dedicate this cookbook to my mother, Dora, who has passed away. Mom, I love you. I remember all the good times we had when I was growing up in Brooklyn. God bless your soul.

Appetizers and Beverages

Broccoli Italian-Style

1 1/4 pounds broccoli
3 tablespoons olive oil
2 tablespoons lemon juice
1 tablespoon chopped fresh parsley
2 cloves garlic, minced
pepper to taste

1. Trim broccoli, discarding tough parts of stems. Cut broccoli into florets with 2-inch stems. Peel remaining broccoli stems and cut into 1/2-inch-thick slices.
2. In a large saucepan, bring 1 quart water to a boil over high heat. Add broccoli and return to a boil. Reduce heat to medium-high. Cook, uncovered, until broccoli is fork-tender. Drain and arrange in a serving dish.
3. In a small bowl, combine oil, lemon juice, parsley, garlic, and pepper.
4. Pour dressing over broccoli, turning to coat. Let stand, covered, 1 to 2 hours before serving to allow flavors to blend.

Note

Choose firm broccoli stems with tight dark-green buds and crisp leaves. Avoid bunches with wilted yellowed leaves. Open buds or tiny yellow flowers indicate overmaturity.

Creamy Spinach Italiano

1 cup ricotta cheese

1/4 cup half-and-half

2 (10-ounce) packages frozen chopped spinach, thawed and squeezed dry

1 1/3 cups French's fried onions, divided

1/2 cup chopped roasted red peppers

1/4 cup chopped fresh basil

1/4 cup grated parmesan cheese

1 teaspoon garlic powder

1/2 teaspoon salt

1. Preheat oven to 350 degrees F. Grease a deep-dish baking pan.
2. In a large bowl, whisk together ricotta and half-and-half until well combined. Stir in spinach, 2/3 cup fried onions, red peppers, basil, parmesan, garlic, and salt.
3. Pour mixture into prepared dish. Bake for 30 minutes or until heated through; stir.
4. Sprinkle with remaining 2/3 cup fried onions. Bake until onions are golden.

Roasted Peppers

Francis DiCandio

mixed yellow, red, and green peppers
minced garlic
pinch salt and pepper
olive oil
chopped fresh parsley

1. Wash peppers, cut off tops, and cut peppers in half, removing seeds and membranes.
2. Place peppers on a baking sheet and broil until skin is blackened and blistered.
3. Place roasted peppers in a plastic bag and let sit for 10 minutes. Remove skin and cut into the size of strips you desire.
4. Place strips in a bowl with garlic, a little salt and pepper, and enough oil to lightly coat. Serve at room temperature.

Chickpea Salad
Francis DiCandio

1 can chickpeas, rinsed well and drained
3 tomatoes, chopped
2 roasted red peppers, chopped
2 tablespoons chopped parsley
2 cloves garlic
1 small red onion
1 1/2 tablespoons olive oil
1 1/2 tablespoons flaxseed oil
salt

1. In a large bowl, combine all ingredients. Toss to coat well.
2. Let stand for at least 20 minutes to allow flavors to blend. Serve cold.

Mussels in Tomato Sauce

Francis DiCandio

3 cloves garlic, very finely chopped
1/3 cup olive oil
1 cup white wine
2 cups canned peeled plum tomatoes, drained and coarsely
chopped
60 mussels, beards removed, scrubbed clean
salt to taste
1/8 teaspoon freshly ground pepper
2 teaspoons chopped parsley

1. In a large saucepan, cook garlic in oil over gentle heat until the bits just begin to take on color. Add wine and reduce over high heat to 1/2 cup.
2. Lower heat, stir in tomatoes, and heat through.
3. Add mussels and steam, covered, until shells open. Discard immediately any that do not open. Transfer mussels, in their shells, to a serving bowl.
4. Season sauce with salt, if needed, and pepper. Pour sauce over mussels and sprinkle with chopped parsley.

Shrimp Sailor-Style

Francis DiCandio

1 small onion, finely chopped
2 cloves garlic, minced
olive oil
2 tablespoons dry white wine
4 cups canned peeled plum tomatoes with juice
1/4 teaspoon oregano
salt and pepper
48 large raw shrimp, shelled and deveined
1 tablespoon finely chopped parsley

1. In a large saucepan over moderate heat, lightly brown onion and garlic in oil. Blend in wine, stirring up cooking glaze at bottom of pan.
2. Add tomatoes with their juice, oregano, and salt and pepper to taste. Continue cooking for 10 minutes.
3. Add shrimp and cook in sauce for 5 minutes. Sprinkle with chopped parsley.

Roasted Chestnuts

Francis DiCandio

2 pounds chestnuts in shell

1. Make a large X in each chestnut with a chestnut knife or sharp paring knife, cutting through the shell.
2. Place chestnuts in a large bowl and cover with cold water. Let soak for 10 minutes and then drain.
3. Heat a large skillet (preferably cast iron) over medium-low heat until hot. Add chestnuts and cook, covered, stirring every few minutes, until skins have pulled back and nuts are tender, 10 to 20 minutes. Serve hot.

Note

Christmas is a time when Italians love to roast chestnuts. This recipe has been in my family for as long as I can remember.

Artichokes Roman-Style

6 artichokes
1 cup breadcrumbs
1/2 cup finely chopped parsley
2 cloves finely chopped garlic
6 anchovy filets in small pieces
4 teaspoons capers, finely chopped
1 tablespoon finely chopped fresh mint leaves
1 egg
1/8 teaspoon white pepper
1/2 cup olive oil, divided
1/2 cup white wine
1/4 cup lemon juice

1. Prepare the artichokes.
2. In a bowl, combine breadcrumbs, parsley, garlic, anchovies, capers, mint, egg, white pepper, and 1/4 cup oil.
3. In a separate bowl, beat together the remaining oil, wine, and lemon juice.
4. Stuff the hollows of each artichokes with 1/8 of the breadcrumb mixture.
5. Blanch artichokes in boiling water for 15 minutes.
6. Arrange artichokes in a deep pot and drizzle leaves of each equally with the wine mixture. Cover pot and cook for 45 minutes or more until you are able to stick a knife into the bottom of the artichokes easily.

Notes

If you like, cool the artichokes and serve them chilled.
You can use the same stuffing to make stuffed peppers.

Tomatoes Stuffed with Tuna

6 large ripe tomatoes
2 cans water-packed tuna, drained and flaked
1/2 cup thinly sliced scallions
1/2 cup thinly sliced celery
1 cup mayonnaise
1 tablespoon thinly chopped parsley
salt and white pepper to taste

1. Cut off tops of tomatoes and scoop out the pulp, leaving a durable shell. Place shells upside down on a plate to drain. Remove seeds from pulp and discard; chop pulp finely.
2. In a mixing bowl, combine tuna, tomato pulp, scallions, celery, mayonnaise, and 1 teaspoon of the parsley. Season with salt and white pepper to taste.
3. Fill tomatoes with tuna mixture; sprinkle tops with remaining parsley. Chill thoroughly before serving.

Sangria

1 pineapple
4 kiwis
2 bananas
1 pint strawberries
1/2 pint blackberries
4 sweet oranges
2 lemons or 5-ounce can grapefruit
4 (750-milliliter) bottles pinot noir
1 (16-ounce) bottle ginger ale

1. Wash all fruit. When cutting fruit, do so in a glass plate to capture all juice that results from cutting.
2. Cut top off pineapple and quarter lengthwise. Set three quarters aside for another use and cut the outer covering off the fourth quarter. Slice into 3/4-inch slices and transfer them and captured juice to a bowl.
3. Peel kiwis and bananas and slice fruit thinly. Transfer to bowl.
4. Remove greenery from strawberries and slice similarly. Remove stems and greenery from blackberries and combine with sliced strawberries. Transfer to bowl.
5. Peel and thinly slice fruit of oranges and lemons. Add to bowl along with all captured juice.
6. Add wine and ginger ale to bowl. Cover with plastic wrap and place in refrigerator for 24 hours.
7. Serve as is or strain, pressing fruit. Recombine strained wine and pressed juice and bottle.

Soups and Salads

Green Bean Salad

Francis DiCandio

1 pound fresh green beans, trimmed
2 tablespoons lemon juice
1 tablespoon extra-virgin olive oil
1/2 teaspoon dried oregano
salt

1. In a medium saucepan, cook beans in boiling salted water for 15 minutes or until tender. Drain well and cool slightly.
2. In a small bowl, whisk together lemon juice, oil, and oregano. Pour over green beans; toss until lightly coated.
3. Cover and refrigerate several hours or overnight before serving. Season to taste with salt.

Tomato and Fresh Mozzarella Salad

🕐 *Francis DiCandio*

1 pound fresh mozzarella cheese, cut into 1/4-inch slices
1 pound ripe tomatoes, cut into 1/4-inch slices
fresh whole large basil leaves, as needed
2 tablespoons olive oil
salt and ground pepper

1. On a serving plate, alternate layers of mozzarella slices, tomato slices, and basil leaves overlapping on a serving plate.
2. Drizzle with oil and sprinkle with salt and pepper.

Note

This dish goes great with a loaf of Italian bread, and don't forget the wine.

Spinach, Nutmeg, and Garlic

🕐 *Francis DiCandio*

4 servings

2 cloves garlic, minced
1 tablespoon extra-virgin olive oil, once around the pan
1 (10- to 12-ounce) bag triple-washed spinach, stems trimmed
pinch salt and black pepper
2 pinches ground nutmeg

1. In a large saucepan, heat garlic in oil over medium heat.
2. Add spinach and turn in pan until leaves wilt. Sprinkle with salt, pepper, and a couple of pinches nutmeg.
3. Remove from heat and serve warm.

Note

This preparation is delicious with any dark greens.

Broth for Poaching Fish

Francis DiCandio

7 cups cold water
1 onion, sliced
1 carrot, sliced
1 stalk celery, sliced
1 bay leaf
5 peppercorns
2 tablespoons vinegar
2 tablespoons salt

1. In a large saucepan, combine all ingredients and cook at a simmer for 15 minutes.

Note:

This will provide sufficient broth to poach 2 pounds shrimps or 12 lobsters.

Lentil Soup
Francis DiCandio

2 tablespoons olive oil
1 small onion, chopped
4 cups beef broth
1 cup dried lentils, rinsed and drained
1/4 cup tomato sauce
1 tablespoon dried Italian herb seasoning
salt and fresh pepper to taste

1. In a large saucepan, heat oil over medium heat until hot. Add onion; cook and stir until softened.
2. Add beef broth and bring mixture to a boil.
3. Stir in lentils, tomato sauce, and Italian seasoning. Cover, reduce heat to low, and simmer for 45 minutes or until tender.
4. Season with salt and pepper. Serve hot.

Chickpea and Shrimp Soup

1 teaspoon olive oil
1 cup diced onion
2 cloves garlic, minced
4 cans beef broth
1 can diced tomatoes
1 can chickpeas, drained
1 can tomato paste
8 (8-ounce) small cooked shrimp
2 teaspoons chopped fresh parsley
1/2 teaspoon salt
1/4 teaspoon pepper

1. In a large saucepan, heat oil over medium high heat. Add onion and garlic; sauté 1 minute.
2. Stir in broth, undrained tomatoes, chickpeas, and tomato paste. Bring to a boil.
3. Reduce heat to low and simmer, uncovered, for 10 minutes.
4. Add shrimp, parsley, salt, and pepper. Simmer 3 minutes or until heated through. Stir before serving.

Tortellini Escarole Soup

1 small head escarole, cored
6 cups chicken broth
8 cheese tortellini (8 ounces in all)
salt and pepper to taste
3/4 cup freshly grated parmesan cheese

1. Rinse escarole in a bowl of water and pat dry. Tear into thin strips.
2. Meanwhile, in a large pot, bring broth and 2 cups water to a boil over medium-high heat.
3. Reduce heat to a medium and add tortellini. Cover and cook until al dente, 4–5 minutes.
4. When tortellini are done, add escarole, salt, and pepper. Simmer under cover until escarole is soft, about 2 minutes. Ladle into soup bowls and add cheese.

antipasti **26**

Vegetables and Side Dishes

Grandma's Zucchini

Francis DiCandio

Serves 6

5 tablespoons olive oil
5 medium zucchini, cut into 1/4-inch-thick rounds
2 cloves garlic, firmly chopped
1/2 teaspoon oregano
2 tablespoons finely chopped parsley
salt and pepper to taste

1. In a skillet, heat oil over high heat. Add zucchini and cook for 10 minutes, stirring rounds constantly so they do not burn.
2. Stir in garlic, oregano, parsley, and salt and pepper to taste. Reduce heat to moderate and continue cooking for 5 minutes more.

Rice Balls with Cheese

3/4 cup well-drained ricotta cheese
salt and white pepper
6 cups boiled rice
3 eggs, beaten
1/4 cup finely chopped dry parsley
1 1/2 cups fine dry breadcrumbs
6 tablespoons olive oil
6 tablespoons butter

1. Season ricotta with salt and white pepper to taste.
2. Shape 3 cups of the rice into 12 cakes, molding each in a 1/4-cup measure.
3. Place 1 tablespoon of the seasoned cheese in the center of each cake. Cover with another cake, similarly shaped, molded from the remaining rice. Press together in the palms of your hands to form a ball, enclosing cheese completely.
4. Dip rice balls into beaten eggs and coat well with parsley and breadcrumbs.
5. In a skillet, heat enough oil and butter (about 2 tablespoons of each) to sauté four rice balls at a time. Add more oil and butter as needed to complete the cooking. Brown well on both sides.

Note

These ricotta rice balls are out of this world.

Pesto Sauce

2 cups basil leaves
1/4 cup pine nuts
2 cloves garlic, crushed
1/2 teaspoon salt
1/4 cup freshly grated encoring cheese
1/2 cup olive oil
pepper to taste
cooked pasta, for serving

1. Place basil, pine nuts, garlic, and salt in a food processor and process for 10 seconds.
2. With the motor running, gradually add oil until a paste is formed. Season with pepper.
3. Add to warm pasta and toss until sauce coats the pasta.

Bolognaise Sauce

2 tablespoons olive oil
2 cloves garlic, crushed
1 onion, chopped
1 carrot, chopped
1 stick celery, chopped
1 pound ground beef
2 cup beef stock
1 cup red wine
2 cans crushed tomatoes, undrained
1 teaspoon sugar
2 tablespoons chopped parsley

1. In a large pan, heat oil. Add garlic, onion, carrot, and celery. Cook, stirring, over low heat until golden, about 5 minutes.
2. Increase heat. Add beef, breaking it up with a fork as it cooks. Stir until well browned.
3. Add remaining ingredients. Bring to a boil, reduce heat, and simmer for 1 1/2 hours, stirring occasionally.

Pasta all'Amatriciana

Serves 4 to 6

2 tablespoons olive oil
2 ounces thick-sliced pancetta, cut into small dice
1 medium onion, finely chopped
1 garlic clove, finely chopped
1 (28- to 35-ounce) can Italian peeled tomatoes, drained and
    chopped
pinch crushed red pepper
salt
1 pound bucatini or perciatelli (pasta)
1/2 cup freshly grated pecorino romano cheese

1. In a skillet or saucepan large enough to hold the cooked pasta, combine oil, pancetta, onion, and garlic. Cook, stirring occasionally, over medium heat until pancetta and onion are golden, about 12 minutes.
2. Stir in tomatoes and crushed red pepper. Add salt to taste. Bring to a simmer and cook, stirring occasionally, until sauce is thickened, about 25 minutes.
3. Meanwhile, in a large pot, bring at least 4 quarts water to a boil. Add pasta and salt to taste. Immediately stir pasta and cook, stirring occasionally, until al dente (tender yet firm to the bite).
4. Scoop out about 1 cup cooking water. Drain pasta and pour into pan with sauce. Toss pasta and sauce together

over high heat for about 1 minute, until pasta is coated. Add a little cooking water if the pasta seems dry.

5. Remove from the heat, add the cheese, and toss well. Serve immediately.

Pastina with Ricotta

Serves 1 or 2

1/2 cup pastina
salt
1/4 cup ricotta
1 teaspoon unsalted butter

1. In a small saucepan, bring about 4 cups water to a boil. Add pastina and salt to taste. Cook, stirring frequently, until the pastina is tender, about 5 minutes.
2. Scoop out some of the cooking water. Drain the pastina and place in a bowl with the ricotta and butter.
3. Mix well, adding a little of the cooking water if the pasta seems dry. Serve immediately.

Zuppa di Cozze

Mussels in Spicy Tomato Sauce

Serves 4

4 pounds mussels (or substitute small clams)
1/3 cup olive oil
4 cloves garlic, very finely chopped, plus 1 whole garlic clove
2 tablespoons chopped fresh flat-leaf parsley
1 small pepperoncino, crumbled, or a pinch of crushed red pepper
1 cup dry white wine
3 pounds ripe tomatoes, peeled, seeded, and chopped, or 2 (28- to 35-ounce) cans Italian peeled tomatoes, drained and chopped
pinch of salt
8 slices Italian bread, toasted

---

1. Place the mussels in cold water to cover for 30 minutes. Drain and scrub with a stiff brush. Scrape off any barnacles or seaweed. Discard any mussels with cracked shells or that do not shut tightly when tapped. Remove the beards by pulling them toward the narrow end of the shells.
2. In a large saucepan, heat oil over low heat. Add chopped garlic, parsley, and pepperoncino over low heat and cook until the garlic is golden, about 1 minute.
3. Stir in wine and bring to a simmer. Add tomatoes and salt. Cook over medium heat, stirring occasionally, until sauce is slightly thickened, about 20 minutes.

4. Gently stir in the mussels. Cover the pot. Cook until mussels open, 5 to 10 minutes. Discard any that refuse to open.
5. Rub the toast with the remaining whole garlic clove. Serve with the mussels.

Mozzarella Cheese Ravioli with Walnuts, Orange Zest, and Thyme

6 tablespoons extra-virgin olive oil, divided

2 sprigs thyme

1/2 cup walnuts, chopped

1 (10-ounce) package Giovanni Rana Mozzarella Cheese Ravioli

zest and juice of one organic orange

salt and pepper to taste

1. In a large skillet, heat 4 tablespoons oil over medium heat. Add thyme sprigs and walnuts and cook until walnuts are fragrant, 2–3 minutes.
2. Cook the ravioli according to package instructions and drain, reserving 1/2 cup of the pasta cooking water.
3. Transfer pasta to pan, adding orange juice and a little of the pasta cooking water to loosen the sauce, if needed.
4. Add remaining oil and the orange zest and toss to combine. Season with salt and pepper to taste. Divide among plates and serve.

Pork Chops with Vinegar Peppers

Serves 4

1 tablespoon olive oil
4 pork rib chops, about 1 inch thick
salt and freshly ground pepper
2 cloves garlic, lightly crushed
2 cups sliced mild pickled peppers, with 2 tablespoons of their
   juice (add a few hot pepperoncini if you like)

---

1. In a large skillet, heat oil over medium-high heat. When oil is very hot, pat chops dry with paper towels. Sprinkle with salt and pepper. Cook chops, turning once, for about 5 minutes on each side, or until browned.
2. Lower heat to medium and scatter garlic around chops. Cover the pan. Cook for 5 to 8 minutes more, or until the chops are just slightly pink when cut near the bone. Do not overcook, or the chops will be dry. Transfer to a plate and keep warm.
3. Add the peppers and the 2 tablespoons liquid to the skillet. Cook, stirring, for 1 to 2 minutes, or until the peppers are just heated through. Spoon the peppers over the chops and serve immediately.

Baked Chicken with Potatoes, Lemon, and Oregano

Serves 4

2 lemons
1 chicken (about 3 1/2 pounds), quartered
3 potatoes, peeled and cut into wedges
1 tablespoon olive oil
1 teaspoon dried oregano
2 cloves garlic, chopped
salt and freshly ground pepper

1. Preheat oven to 450 degrees F.
2. Squeeze juice from 1 lemon and slice the other.
3. In a large baking pan, arrange chicken and potatoes in a single layer. Sprinkle with lemon juice, oil, oregano, garlic, and salt and pepper to taste. Turn pieces to coat evenly, then turn chicken skin-side up. Tuck lemon slices and potatoes in between the chicken pieces.
4. Bake chicken for 45 minutes. Baste with pan juices. Continue to bake, basting occasionally, for 15 to 30 minutes longer, or until chicken is browned and potatoes are tender.
5. Transfer chicken, potatoes, and lemon slices to a serving platter. Tip pan and skim off fat. Pour juices over the chicken and serve.

Tuna Salad with Green Beans and Tomatoes

Serves 2

1 (7-ounce) can tuna packed in olive oil
2 medium tomatoes, cut into bite-size pieces
2 hard-cooked eggs, peeled and quartered
3 or 4 thin slices red onion, quartered
pinch dried oregano
1 to 2 tablespoons fresh lemon juice
salt and freshly ground pepper
8 ounces green beans, cooked and cut into bite-size pieces
lemon wedges

1. Place tuna, with its oil, in a large bowl. Break into pieces with a fork.
2. Add tomatoes, eggs, and onion. Sprinkle with oregano, lemon juice, a pinch of salt, and pepper to taste. Toss gently.
3. Arrange green beans on a platter. Top with tuna salad. Garnish with lemon wedges and serve immediately.

Chicken and Roasted Garlic Ravioli with Green Beans, Bacon, and Almonds

1/4 cup slivered almonds

1/4 cup butter

1/2 cup diced bacon

1 (10-ounce) package Giovanni Rana Chicken and Roasted Garlic Ravioli

1 heaped cup fresh or frozen green beans, cut into 2-inch lengths

salt and pepper

grated or shaved parmigiano-reggiano cheese (optional)

1. In a skillet, toss almonds over medium high heat until golden, 2–3 minutes. Set aside.
2. In a separate large skillet, melt the butter. Add bacon and cook until crispy, 3–4 minutes.
3. Meanwhile, cook ravioli according to package instructions. If using fresh green beans, add to the water at the same time as the pasta. If using frozen, add during the last 2 minutes of cooking.
4. Drain ravioli and green beans, reserving 1/2 cup of the pasta cooking water. Add ravioli and beans to skillet with bacon. Toss gently and season with salt and pepper to taste.
5. Divide ravioli mixture among plates, sprinkle with toasted almonds, and serve, topped with cheese if desired.

Chicken Francese

Serves 4

1 pound thin-sliced chicken cutlets
salt and freshly ground pepper
2 large eggs
1/2 cup all-purpose flour
1/2 cup chicken broth
1/4 cup dry white wine
2 to 3 tablespoons fresh lemon juice (to taste)
3 tablespoons olive oil
3 tablespoons unsalted butter
1 tablespoon chopped fresh flat-leaf parsley
lemon wedges

1. Place chicken cutlets between two sheets of plastic wrap. With a meat pounder or mallet, gently pound slices to about a 1/4-inch thickness. Sprinkle generously with salt and pepper.
2. In a shallow bowl, beat eggs with salt and pepper until well blended. Spread flour on a plate.
3. In a measuring cup or bowl, mix together broth, wine, and lemon juice.
4. In a large skillet, heat oil with butter over medium heat until sizzling.
5. Dip only enough of the cutlets in the flour as will fit in the pan in a single layer, then dip in the egg. Add to pan and cook for 2 to 3 minutes per side, or until golden brown. Regulate the heat so the butter does not burn. Transfer

chicken to a plate and keep warm. Repeat with remaining chicken.

6. When all of the chicken is done, add broth mixture to the pan. Raise heat and cook, scraping the bottom of the pan, until sauce is slightly thickened. Stir in parsley.

7. Return chicken pieces to the skillet and turn once or twice in the sauce. Serve immediately with lemon wedges.

Struffoli

I remember my brother-in-law John Zerga making these honey balls at Christmastime—the good old days!

Serves 12

1 1/2 cups all-purpose flour, more as needed
1/4 teaspoon salt
3 large eggs
vegetable oil for deep-frying
1 1/2 cups honey
chopped candied orange peel, red and green candied cherries, multicolored candy sprinkles, or toasted sliced almonds

1. In a large bowl, combine flour and salt. Add eggs and stir until well blended.
2. Turn dough out onto a lightly floured board and knead until smooth, about 5 minutes; add a little more flour if the dough seems sticky.
3. Shape dough into a ball and cover with an overturned bowl. Let rest for 30 minutes.
4. Cut dough into 8 pieces. Roll one piece under your palms into a 1/2-inch-thick rope. Cut the rope into 1/2-inch pieces. If dough feels sticky, use a tiny bit of flour to dust the board or your hands; don't coat with flour, or the oil will foam up when you fry the struffoli.
5. Pour about 2 inches oil into a deep heavy saucepan or a deep fryer. Heat oil to 370 degrees F on a deep-frying thermometer or until a small bit of the dough dropped

into the oil sizzles, swims rapidly around the pan, and turns brown in 1 minute.

6. Being careful not to splash the hot oil, slip just enough of the dough pieces into the pan as will fit without crowding. Cook, stirring once or twice, until the struffoli are crisp and evenly golden brown, 1 to 2 minutes. Remove with a slotted spoon and drain on paper towels. Continue with the remaining dough.

7. When all of the struffoli are fried, gently heat honey just to a simmer in a large shallow saucepan. Remove from heat, add struffoli, and stir well.

8. Pile struffoli on a serving plate. Decorate with candied fruits, sprinkles, or nuts. These keep well covered at room temperature for several days.

9. To serve, break off portions of the struffoli with two large spoons or a salad server.

Pasta e Fagioli

Pasta Fazool ∽ Pasta and Beans

Serves 8

8 ounces (1 cup) dried cannellini or Great Northern beans
1/4 cup olive oil
1 rib celery, chopped
2 cloves garlic, lightly crushed
1 cup peeled, seeded, and chopped fresh tomatoes or canned
 Italian peeled tomatoes
1 teaspoon tomato paste
1/2 cup water
1 small dried pepperoncino, crumbled, or pinch of crushed
 red pepper
salt
8 ounces ditalini or spaghetti or other pasta, broken into
 1-inch pieces

1. Put beans in a bowl with cold water to cover by 1 inch and
 let stand for at least 4 hours or overnight in the refrigerator.
 Add more water if necessary to keep the beans covered.
2. Drain beans and place in a pot with fresh water to cover
 by 1/2 inch. Bring to a simmer over low heat. Cover and
 cook until beans are very soft, about 1 hour. Add more
 water if needed to keep beans just covered.
3. When beans are almost ready, heat oil in a large saucepan
 over moderate heat. Add celery and garlic. When garlic
 is golden, discard it. Add tomatoes, tomato paste, water,

pepperoncino, and salt to taste. Simmer for 10 minutes or until sauce is slightly thickened.

4. Add beans and their cooking liquid. Bring the mixture to a simmer, mashing some of the beans with the back of a large spoon.

5. Stir in pasta and cook, stirring often, until pasta is al dente, tender yet still firm to the bite. The mixture should be very thick, but add a little boiling water if it seems too thick. Turn off the heat and let stand for 10 minutes before serving.

Note

You can use 3 cups canned beans, rinsed and drained, in place of the dried beans. Skip the first two steps and add beans in step 4.

Shrimp Scampi

Serves 2

4 tablespoons unsalted butter

2 tablespoons olive oil

3 large cloves garlic, minced

16 large shrimp, shelled and deveined

pinch of salt

2 tablespoons very finely chopped fresh flat-leaf parsley, plus
a few sprigs for garnish

1 tablespoon fresh lemon juice

lemon wedges

1. In a large skillet, melt butter with oil over medium-low heat. When butter foam subsides, stir in garlic. Cook, stirring occasionally, until garlic is lightly golden, about 7 minutes. Do not let garlic brown.
2. Increase the heat to medium high and add shrimp and salt. Cook for 2 to 3 minutes, turning shrimp once, until they are just pink. Stir in parsley and lemon juice and cook 1 minute more.
3. Serve garnished with lemon wedges and parsley sprigs.

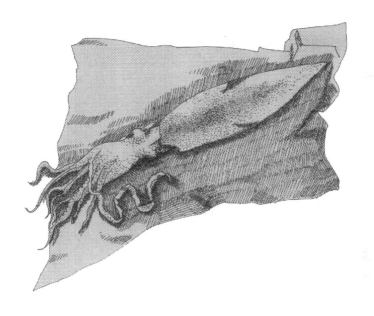

Braciole

Stuffed Beef Rolls in Tomato Sauce

Serves 4

4 thin slices boneless beef round (about 1 pound)
1 clove garlic, finely chopped, plus 2 cloves garlic, lightly crushed (divided)
2 tablespoons freshly grated pecorino romano cheese
2 tablespoons chopped fresh flat-leaf parsley
salt and freshly ground pepper
4 thin slices prosciutto
2 tablespoons olive oil
1 cup dry red wine
4 cups tomato puree, or canned Italian tomatoes passed through a food mill
4 fresh basil leaves, torn into small pieces
1 pound ziti or penne, cooked and still hot

1. Place beef between two pieces of plastic wrap and pound gently with a meat pounder or rubber mallet to a 1/4- to 1/8-inch thickness.
2. Sprinkle beef with chopped garlic, cheese, parsley, and salt and pepper. Cover with prosciutto slices. Roll up each piece like a sausage and tie it with kitchen string.
3. In a large pot, heat oil. Add braciole and crushed garlic. Cook, turning meat occasionally, until meat is browned on all sides and garlic is golden. Add wine and simmer for 2 minutes. Remove and discard crushed garlic.

4. Stir in tomato puree and basil. Cover and cook over low heat, turning meat occasionally, until it is tender when pierced with a fork, about 2 hours. Add a little water if the sauce becomes too thick.

5. Serve sauce over hot cooked ziti as a first course, followed by braciole.

Spaghetti Puttanesca

Serves 4 to 6

3 cloves garlic, finely chopped
1 small pepperoncino, crumbled, or a pinch of crushed red pepper
1/3 cup olive oil
2 1/2 pounds ripe plum tomatoes, peeled, seeded, and chopped, or 1 (28- to 35-ounce) can Italian peeled tomatoes, drained and chopped
1 teaspoon dried oregano
salt
1/2 cup pitted and chopped oil-cured olives
1/4 cup capers, rinsed
8 to 12 anchovy fillets, drained
1/4 cup finely chopped fresh flat-leaf parsley
1 pound spaghetti

1. In a skillet large enough to hold the sauce and cooked pasta, cook garlic and pepperoncino in oil over low heat until garlic is golden. Raise heat to medium and add tomatoes, oregano, and a pinch of salt. Cook for 15 to 20 minutes, or until sauce is thickened.
2. Stir in olives, capers, anchovies, and parsley; cook 2 minutes more.
3. Meanwhile, in a large pot, bring at least 4 quarts of water to a boil. Add salt to taste and spaghetti. Cook, stirring frequently, until pasta is al dente, tender yet still firm to the bite. Drain and add to simmering sauce.
4. Toss well. Serve immediately.

Arugula and Parmesan Salad

Serves 2

1 bunch arugula, washed and dried
2 tablespoons extra-virgin olive oil
2 teaspoons balsamic vinegar
salt and freshly ground pepper
small piece parmigiano-reggiano cheese

1. Cut off arugula stems. Tear leaves into bite-size pieces.
2. In a large bowl, whisk together oil, vinegar, and salt and pepper to taste. Add arugula and toss well. Pile salad onto two plates.
3. With a vegetable peeler, shave cheese over salad. Serve immediately.

Main Dishes

Italian Meatballs

Francis DiCandio

2 cups olive oil
1 pound chopped meat chuck
1/4 cup chopped parsley
1/4 cup grated cheese
4 slices white bread, crusts removed, soaked in 1 cup water
   and then squeezed dry
3 cloves garlic, minced
2 eggs
1 cup water
pinch black pepper
pinch salt

1. In a frying pan, heat enough oil to go halfway up the meatballs.
2. In a large bowl, mix together remaining ingredients. Form mixture into meatballs.
3. Add meatballs to frying pan. Fry until edges are crusty and then turn. Repeat with other side and remove.

Note

Don't overmix meatball mixture.

Chicken Marsala

Francis DiCandio

1 tablespoon butter
2 boneless skinless chicken breasts
1 cup sliced carrots
1 cup sliced mushrooms
1/3 cup chicken stock
1/3 cup marsala cooking wine

1. In a skillet, melt butter over medium high heat. Add chicken and cook 5 minutes.
2. Turn chicken over and add remaining ingredients. Bring to a boil and then simmer 15 to 20 minutes until juices run clear.

Lemon Chicken with Olives

2 tablespoons all-purpose flour
2 teaspoons grated lemon zest
1/2 teaspoon ground cumin
kosher salt and pepper
1 1/2 pounds chicken esculents (6 to 8)
2 tablespoons olive oil (divided)
2 shallots, thinly sliced
1 cup pitted green olives, halved
1/2 cup fresh flat-leaf parsley chopped
1/2 cup dry white wine
1 tablespoon fresh lemon juice

1. On a plate, combine flour, lemon zest, cumin, and 1/2 teaspoon each salt and pepper. Add chicken and coat with flour mixture, tapping off any excess.
2. In a large skillet, heat 1 tablespoon oil over medium-high heat. Add chicken and cook in two batches until golden, 2 to 3 minutes per side. Transfer to a plate.
3. Wipe out skillet and heat remaining 1 tablespoon oil over medium heat. Add shallots and cook until soft, 5 to 7 minutes. Add olives, parsley, wine, and lemon juice; bring to a boil.
4. Nestle chicken in vegetables. Simmer, covered, until chicken is cooked through, 4 to 6 minutes.

Chicken Cacciatore

Cacciatore is the Italian word for "hunter," and it's said that this dish originated with hunters who prepared their game in the field with whatever other ingredients were at hand. They'd throw poultry or rabbit in a pot with onions, tomatoes, herbs, and maybe some carrots, bell peppers, or mushrooms. They would pour in some wine and set the pot in the fire to braise low and slow. The result is fall-off-the-bone tender. This is a stovetop recipe, but you can prepare it in a slow cooker too.

1 chicken (3 to 4 pounds), cut up into parts, or an equal weight of precut bone-in parts

3/4 cup all-purpose flour

1 teaspoon salt, plus more for seasoning

1/2 teaspoon freshly ground black pepper, plus more for seasoning

1/4 cup olive oil

1 large onion, halved and sliced into very thin crescents

3/4 cup dry white wine

2 cloves garlic, minced

1 teaspoon fresh sage, chopped

1 teaspoon fresh thyme, chopped

1 medium carrot, diced

2 celery stalks, sliced into thin crescents

1 red, yellow, or orange bell pepper, seeded, deribbed, and diced

1/2 cup white or cremini mushrooms, sliced

1 (28-ounce) can tomatoes with juice, diced

1. Rinse chicken parts and pat dry. Combine flour, salt, and black pepper on a plate and spread out. Dredge chicken parts in the flour to coat thoroughly but lightly, shaking off excess.

2. In a large pot over medium-high heat, heat oil until hot but not smoking. Add chicken, skin-side down, and brown it; then flip over and brown the other side. You may have to do this in batches. Set the browned chicken aside.

3. Reduce heat to medium and add onion. Sauté until golden, about 10 minutes.

4. Pour in wine and deglaze the pot, scraping any brown bits from the bottom and sides into the liquid. Add garlic, sage, thyme, carrot, celery, bell pepper, and mushrooms; simmer until carrot is tender but not soft.

5. Add tomatoes, season with salt and black pepper, and simmer, uncovered, for 10 minutes.

6. Return chicken to pot and bring sauce to a simmer. Reduce heat to low and cover pot. Cook for 40 minutes, then check the largest piece of chicken for doneness. If it needs to cook longer, stir and cover the pot. Check again after 5 minutes and repeat until chicken is fully cooked.

7. Remove chicken to a platter and continue to simmer the sauce, if necessary, until any wateriness evaporates. To serve, spoon sauce over the chicken.

Scalloped Chicken or Veal

In the francese, parmigiana, piccata, and marsala recipes that follow, chicken or veal work equally well; make your choice based on your own tastes. Thin fillets of chicken or veal are called scallops or, in Italian, *scallopine*, and they are prepared the same way for each of the recipes. If you're using chicken, use skinless, boneless breasts; each will yield two cutlets, which equal two servings. Even easier is to buy presliced cutlets in your supermarket, about ¼ pound per serving. If you're using veal, the cutlets will also come presliced. Veal cutlets tend to be smaller than chicken, so you may need more than one per serving.

1 pound boneless, skinless chicken breasts, chicken cutlets, or veal cutlets
½ cup all-purpose flour
1 ½ teaspoons salt
½ teaspoon freshly ground pepper
3 tablespoons unsalted butter
4 tablespoons olive oil

1. To make chicken cutlets, first rinse meat and pat dry. Cut breasts in half sandwich-wise. Butterfly them open and separate the halves. Place chicken or veal cutlets between pieces of plastic wrap and gently use a meat hammer or rolling pin to flatten them to ¼-inch thickness.
2. Combine flour, salt, and pepper on a plate. Dredge each piece of chicken or veal on both sides, shaking off excess. Place in a single layer on a clean plate and set aside.

3. Cover another clean plate with a double layer of paper towels.
4. In a large skillet over medium-high heat, melt butter into olive oil until hot but not smoking. Place half the cutlets in the pan in a single layer and brown on both sides, about 1 minute per side. Remove to the paper-towel-covered plate and repeat for the rest of the cutlets. Use these in the recipes that follow.

Veal Scaloppine

🌐 *Francis DiCandio*

pinch salt and pepper
1/4 cup lemon juice
4 (1/4-inch) veal cutlets
3 tablespoons olive oil
flour, for dredging
1 slice whole lemon
1 cup dry white wine
1/2 cup chicken stock
10 capers

1. Sprinkle salt, pepper, and lemon juice over veal cutlets.
2. In a large skillet, heat oil. Dredge veal in flour and add to skillet. Cook 1 or 2 minutes on each side until bounced. Remove veal.
3. Add lemon, wine, and stock and bring to a boil. Cook until thickened.
4. Returned the veal to pan, coat with the sauce, and heat through. Add capers before serving.

Baked Clams Oreganata

Do not purchase clams with damaged shells or shells that are not tightly shut. Before cooking, recheck clams and discard any that have opened. You should end up with at least 16 live clams.

20 live littleneck clams
3/4 cup plain breadcrumbs
3 tablespoons freshly grated parmigiano-reggiano cheese
2 cloves garlic, finely chopped
1 tablespoon fresh oregano, chopped, or 2 teaspoons dried
2 tablespoons fresh parsley, chopped, or 2 teaspoons dried
1/4 cup extra-virgin olive oil, plus more for finishing
salt and freshly ground black pepper
1 lemon, cut into 8 wedges

1. Move broiler pan to middle rung under the broiler. Preheat oven to 450 degrees F.
2. Scrub clams under cold running water to remove any barnacles, seaweed, and sand. Place on a baking sheet in a single layer.
3. Bake clams in oven (not broiler) until they just start to open, 2 to 3 minutes. Remove from oven and let cool until they can be handled. Discard any clams that have not opened.
4. Turn oven to broil. Working over a small bowl to catch the clam juice, hold a clam in the palm of one hand and use a butter knife to pry it open. Discard top shell and carefully detach meat from bottom shell. Strain clam juice

through cheesecloth or a very fine sieve to get rid of any sand or other debris.

5. In a medium mixing bowl, toss breadcrumbs, cheese, garlic, oregano, and parsley until just combined. Stir in oil and 2 tablespoons clam juice. Season with salt and pepper.

6. Use a tablespoon to top clams with the crumb mixture. Pat crumbs down gently so they stay in place (but don't pack them) and drizzle with oil. Place clams on the broiler pan and broil until topping is crisp and golden brown, 4 to 5 minutes.

7. Serve with lemon wedges on the side.

Mussels Fra Diavolo

Fra diavolo (Italian for "brother devil") was an eighteenth-century guerilla who fought the French occupiers of the southern Italian city of Naples. Originated by Italian immigrants to the United States, the sauce that bears his name is as hot and fiery as he was.

1 batch pomodoro sauce (see recipe, page 3)
1 1/2 teaspoons red pepper flakes, crushed
3 red chiles, dried
1 (8-ounce) bottle clam juice
1 1/2 cups dry white wine, divided
salt and freshly ground black pepper
5 pounds live mussels
1 tablespoon olive oil
3 shallots, finely chopped

1. In a large saucepan over medium-high heat, combine pomodoro sauce, red pepper flakes, dried chiles, clam juice, and 1/2 cup wine. Season with salt and black pepper.
2. Bring sauce to a boil, partially cover the pot, and lower heat to medium low. Simmer sauce for 30 to 45 minutes, stirring occasionally.
3. While sauce is cooking, check mussels to make sure they are alive: pick them up, squeeze gently, and tap on a work surface. Discard any that do not close when squeezed or tapped. Hold each live mussel in your hand and, with a dish towel or paper towel, sharply tug the clump of

hairs—the beard—down toward the hinge of the shell to pull it off.

4. Scrub mussels under cold running water to remove any barnacles, seaweed, and sand. Put each mussel in a mixing bowl filled with cold water; if it floats, discard it. Immediately remove live mussels from water; you should end up with at least 4 pounds. Store mussels in the refrigerator, covered with a damp towel, until you are ready to cook them.

5. In a wide saucepan with high sides, heat oil over medium heat and add shallots. Cook for 1 minute, stirring constantly.

6. Stir in remaining cup of wine and sauce mixture. Bring to a boil and add mussels. Stir to coat, cover pot, and cook until shells open, 3 to 5 minutes. Discard any mussels that have not opened.

7. Transfer mussels to four large individual bowls and spoon sauce over the top. Serve with an additional large bowl for discarding empty shells while eating.

Note

Do not purchase mussels with damaged shells. The freshest mussels tend to be tightly closed, but open shells do not necessarily mean mussels are dead. Store live mussels in a large, dry mixing bowl in the refrigerator, covered with a damp towel so they can breathe, until you are ready to use them.

Orecchiette with Sausage and Broccoli Rabe

The dark-green bitterness of the broccoli rabe, the crumbly savoriness of the sausage, and the robust texture of the pasta make this a quintessential Italian dish.

1 1/2 pounds hot Italian sausage
1/4 cup extra-virgin olive oil
3 cloves garlic, minced
2 bunches broccoli rabe, destemmed and roughly chopped
1/2 cup white wine
salt and freshly ground black pepper
1 pound dried orecchiette, cooked to al dente according to package directions
1/2 cup freshly grated parmigiano-reggiano or pecorino romano cheese, plus more for sprinkling

1. Slit sausage casings lengthwise and scrape stuffing into a small mixing bowl. Cover and set aside.
2. In a large skillet, heat oil with garlic over medium heat until garlic sizzles but does not brown. When pan is hot, add sausage meat and cook, stirring to break up clumps, until sausage browns, about 5 minutes.
3. Add broccoli rabe and continue cooking until greens are crisp yet tender.
4. Pour in wine and deglaze pan, scraping brown bits off the bottom. Simmer until broccoli is fully tender but not soft. Season with salt and pepper.

5. Add orecchiette to pan and toss to coat. Sprinkle cheese onto the pasta and toss until all ingredients are well combined. Serve immediately with cheese on the side.

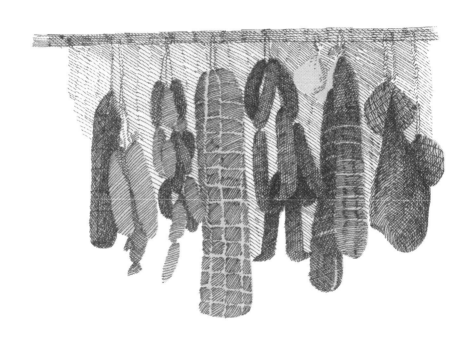

Tagliatelle al Prosciutto

pasta
3 1/2 tablespoons butter
6 ounces parma ham
1 small onion, finely chopped
pinch salt and milled black pepper
3/4 cup grated parmesan cheese

1. Boil a large pot of salted water. Add pasta and cook until al dente.
2. In a large pan, melt butter. Add ham and sauté.
3. Add onion and sauté until transparent.
4. Drain pasta well and add to the pan. Mix very well. Add pepper and cheese before serving.

Stuffed Shells
Francis DiCandio

2 cups pasta sauce (divided)
2 pounds ricotta cheese
2 cups shredded mozzarella cheese
1/4 cup grated parmesan cheese
3 eggs
1 tablespoon chopped fresh parsley
1/8 teaspoon black pepper
1 box jumbo pasta shells, cooked and drained

1. Preheat oven to 350 degrees F.
2. In a 13-by-9-inch baking pan, evenly spread 1 cup of sauce.
3. In a large bowl, combine cheeses, eggs, parsley, and black pepper.
4. Fill shells with cheese mixture and arrange in prepared baking pan. Evenly top with remaining sauce. Bake 45 minutes.

Note

Pasta should always be cooked in plenty of water at a fast boil. This allows the pasta to circulate during cooking so that all of it will be evenly cooked.

Prosciutto and Cheese Tortelloni with Celery, Crème Fraîche, and Breadcrumbs

2 tablespoons butter or extra-virgin olive oil
1/4 cup breadcrumbs
a few sprigs thyme
3 tablespoons grated parmigiano-reggiano cheese
salt and pepper to taste
1 (10-ounce) package Giovanni Rana Prosciutto and Cheese
    Tortelloni
1/2 cup crème fraîche
1 celery heart, sliced, leaves chopped

1. In a large skillet, heat the butter. Add the breadcrumbs and sauté for a few minutes until lightly golden and fragrant.
2. Pour breadcrumbs into a bowl and set aside; when cold, add thyme leaves, grated cheese, salt, and pepper; mix well.
3. Cook tortelloni according to package instructions and drain, reserving 1/4 cup of the pasta cooking water.
4. Meanwhile, in a large skillet, heat crème fraîche over medium heat. Add pasta, season with salt and pepper to taste, and toss to combine, adding a little of the pasta cooking water to loosen the sauce if needed.
5. Divide tortelloni between two plates, sprinkle with celery and breadcrumb mixture, and serve.

Ravioli with Herbs

Francis DiCandio

2 tablespoons olive oil

1 clove garlic, halved

1 box or bag ravioli

1 tablespoon butter

2 tablespoons chopped parsley

1/3 cup chopped basil

2 tablespoons chopped chives

1. In a small bowl, combine oil and garlic; set aside.
2. In a large pan, bring water to a rapid boil. Add ravioli and cook until tender. Drain well and return to pan.
3. Discard garlic and add oil to pasta. Add butter and herbs; toss well.

Chickpea Pasta with Almonds and Parmesan

1 tablespoon olive oil

3 cloves garlic, chopped

7 cups low-sodium vegetable or chicken stock

1/2 teaspoon crushed red pepper

kosher salt

12 ounces angel-hair pasta

1 can chickpeas, rinsed

1 cup fresh flat-leaf parsley, chopped

1/2 cup grated parmesan cheese

1/2 cup chopped roasted almonds

1. In a large saucepan, heat oil over medium-high heat. Add garlic and cook, stirring, for 1 minute.
2. Add stock, red pepper, and 3/4 teaspoons salt to saucepan; bring to a boil. Add pasta and cook, stirring occasionally, until stock is nearly absorbed and pasta is al dente, about 6 minutes.
3. Stir in parmesan and almonds before serving.

pasta

1/2 cup olive oil

3 rashers bacon, chopped

1 onion, chopped

1/3 lemon juice

1 tablespoon thyme leaves

tomatoes

1/3 cup pine nuts, toasted

1. In a large pan, bring water to a rapid boil. Add pasta, cook until tender, and drain.
2. In a separate large pan, heat oil. Add bacon and onion and stir over medium heat for 5 minutes or until bacon is brown and onion has softened.
3. Add pasta to pan along with lemon juice, thyme, tomatoes, and pine nuts. Stir over low heat for 2 minutes or until heated through.

Spaghetti and Garlic
In memory of my mother

1 pound spaghetti
1/3 cup extra-virgin olive oil
5 cloves garlic, minced
1/4 tablespoon or two pinches red pepper
handful flat-leaf parsley, chopped
black pepper to taste

1. Cook spaghetti in plenty of boiling salted water.
2. In a frying pan, heat oil with garlic and pepper flakes. Cook until garlic is a little brown.
3. Drain pasta and toss into same pan. Add parsley and black pepper.

Note

This recipe is in memory of my mother, Dora. I remember that when I was growing up in Brooklyn, my mother would make this dish all the time. God bless her soul.

Spaghetti with Fresh Tomato Sauce

Francis DiCandio

4 spring onions (scallions), chopped
4 firm ripe tomatoes, chopped into small pieces
8 green olives, chopped
2 tablespoons capers, chopped
2 cloves garlic, crushed
1/2 teaspoon dried oregano
1/3 cup parsley, chopped
1/3 cup olive oil
1 box spaghetti

1. In a large bowl, combine all ingredients except spaghetti and mix well. Cover and refrigerate for at least 2 hours.
2. In a large pan, bring water to a rapid boil. Add pasta and cook until tender. Drain and return to pan.
3. Add cold sauce to hot pasta and mix well.

Spaghetti with Pesto

1 tablespoon pine nuts

1 1/2 bunches fresh basil, leaves plucked, rinsed, dried, and coarsely chopped

1 clove garlic, peeled and coarsely chopped

pinch salt

3 tablespoons grated parmesan cheese

1/4 cup olive oil

pinch pepper

1 pound spaghetti

1. In a dry pan, toast the pine nuts.
2. In a food processor or blender, work pine nuts, basil, garlic, and a little salt to a paste. Mix in parmesan and olive oil; season with pepper.
3. Cook spaghetti in ample salted water until al dente. Drain and toss with the pesto. Serve immediately.

Spaghetti Parmesan

1/2 cup olive oil
1 clove garlic, finely chopped
4 large tomatoes, chopped
2 tablespoons finely chopped parsley
2 teaspoons finely chopped basil
salt and pepper
1 1/2 pounds spaghetti
6 ounces shredded mozzarella cheese
1/2 cup grated parmesan cheese

---

1. Preheat oven to 350 degrees F. Lightly oil a baking dish.
2. In a saucepan, heat olive oil. Add garlic and sauté until it takes on a little color.
3. Add tomatoes, parsley, basil, and salt and pepper to taste. Cook, covered, over moderate heat for 10 minutes.
4. Meanwhile, cook spaghetti as directed on package. Drain and spread hot spaghetti in prepared baking dish; pour sauce over.
5. Combine cheeses and sprinkle evenly over sauce. Bake until cheeses melt and are lightly browned. Serve at once.

Spaghetti with Zucchini and Garlic

2 small zucchini
1/4 cup extra-virgin olive oil
4 cloves garlic, finely chopped
salt and pepper to taste
1 pound spaghetti
1/2 cup grated parmigiano-reggiano cheese

1. Pile up two or three layers of paper towels on a work surface. Using a box grater, hold one zucchini at a time at an angle and shred onto towels.
2. Heat a large skillet over moderate heat. Add oil and then chopped garlic. When garlic speaks by sizzling in oil, add shredded zucchini; season with salt and pepper. Sauté 7–10 minutes.
3. Cook spaghetti according to package instructions. Drain and add to pan.
4. Toss spaghetti with zucchini and grated cheese. Adjust seasonings and serve.

Spaghetti Caruso-Style

2 tablespoons olive oil
1 medium onion, thinly sliced
3 cup canned peeled plum tomatoes
1 small bay leaf
1/4 teaspoon dried oregano
4 tablespoons butter, divided
1/4 pound fresh mushrooms, thinly sliced
salt and pepper
1 1/2 pounds spaghetti
1 pound chicken livers
2 tablespoons dry white wine
1 tablespoon finely chopped parsley
grated parmesan cheese

1. In a saucepan, heat olive oil. Add onion and brown lightly.
2. Add tomatoes, bay leaf, and oregano. Cook, covered, at simmer for 20 minutes.
3. In a skillet, heat 2 tablespoons butter. Add mushrooms and cook briskly until slices begin to take on a color.
4. Add tomato mixture and continue cooking for 10 minutes. Season with salt and pepper to taste.

Baked Spaghetti Frittata

1 tablespoon butter

5 mushrooms, sliced

1 capsicum pepper, seeded and chopped

4 ham, sliced

1/2 cup frozen peas

6 eggs

1 cup milk

salt and pepper

1/2 pound spaghetti, cooked and chopped

2 tablespoons chopped fresh parsley

1/4 cup grated parmesan cheese

1. Preheat oven to 360 degrees F. Grease a 9-inch baking dish.
2. In a frying pan, melt butter. Add mushrooms and cook over low heat, 2–3 minutes.
3. Add capsicum and cook 1 minute. Stir in ham and peas. Remove pan from heat and allow mixture to cool slightly.
4. In a large bowl, whisk together eggs and milk. Season with salt and pepper to taste.
5. Add spaghetti, parsley, and mushroom mixture to bowl and stir.
6. Pour mixture into prepared dish and sprinkle with cheese. Bake for 25–30 minutes.

Note

Food from Italy comes from three regions: northern, central, and southern.

Penne with Pancetta, Onion, and Tomato

8 ounces penne
1/4 cup olive oil
1 small clove garlic, slice thin
1/2 cup diced pancetta, cooked
1/2 cup thin-sliced onion
1 pinch chopped fresh rosemary
2 large pinches kosher salt
1 pinch crushed red pepper
fresh black pepper
2 1/2 cups crushed tomatoes
1 tablespoon butter
1/4 cup chopped parsley
1/4 cup grated parmesan cheese

1. Bring a large pot of salted water to a boil. Add penne and cook until al dente, about 10 minutes. Drain.
2. While pasta is cooking, heat oil in a large saucepan. Add garlic and sauté until golden.
3. Add pancetta (along with its juices) and onion. Sauté 3–4 minutes or until onion is soft.
4. Add rosemary and crushed red pepper and stir for 30 seconds. Add tomatoes and simmer for 6–7 minutes.
5. Swirl butter into sauce. Add drained pasta and cook over low heat for 2 minutes or until sauce is slightly absorbed by the pasta.
6. Sprinkle in parsley and cheese, toss together, and serve.

Penne alla Vodka

3 tablespoons unsalted butter
2 large cloves garlic, finely chopped
2 ounces thinly sliced prosciutto
1 can Italian tomatoes, drained
1/2 teaspoon crushed red pepper
1/2 cup heavy cream
1/4 cup vodka
pinch salt
1 pound penne
1/2 cup grated parmigiano-reggiano cheese

1. In a skillet large enough to hold the cooked pasta, melt butter over medium heat. Add garlic and cook until golden, about 2 minutes.
2. Stir in prosciutto and cook for 1 minute Add tomatoes and crushed red pepper and simmer for 5 minutes.
3. Stir in cream and cook, stirring, for 1 minute. Add vodka and cook for 2 minutes. Season to taste with salt.
4. Meanwhile, bring at least 4 quarts of water to a boil in a large pot. Add pasta and salt to taste. Cook, stirring frequently, until penne is al dente—tender yet still firm to the bite. Drain, reserving some of the water.
5. Add the pasta to skillet with sauce and toss until well coated. Add a little of the reserved cooking water if sauce seems too thick.
6. Add cheese and toss again. Serve immediately.

Basic Risotto

Risotto is kind of like an upscale version of rice pilaf, that predictable side dish served next to vegetable medleys in chain restaurants. It's cooked in a broth for flavor and may include a variety of ingredients, such as wine, herbs, vegetables, or seafood. But risotto ain't no Rice-A-Roni! It's a masterpiece of northern Italian cookery—a sophisticated dish of subtle flavors, well-integrated ingredients, and uniquely creamy texture that comes from the very special rice from which it's made. Risotto, such as this classic rendition, is typically served as a *primi*, but more substantial versions are often served as a main course.

1 quart low-sodium beef, chicken, or vegetable broth
5 tablespoons unsalted butter
1 small onion, very finely chopped
2 cups arborio rice
3/4 cup freshly grated parmigiano-reggiano cheese
salt

1. In a medium saucepan over medium-high heat, bring broth plus 1 cup water to a simmer. Reduce heat to medium low and keep the broth simmering while you cook the risotto.
2. In a large saucepan over medium-high heat, melt butter until it foams. Add onion and sauté until it is translucent but not brown, about 2 minutes.
3. Add rice and stir to toast it and coat it with the butter, 3 to 4 minutes.

4. Keep heat at medium and ladle 1/2 cup hot broth into pot with rice. With a long wooden spoon, stir without stopping, frequently scraping down the sides of the pot and scraping off the bottom to keep rice from sticking. When rice has absorbed the broth, after about 3 minutes, add another 1/2 cup liquid and repeat process.

5. Continue the routine, stirring constantly, for another 15 minutes, then start checking the texture of the rice. If it is not yet al dente, keep adding liquid and stirring as you have been. Check the texture every few minutes. If you run out of broth before the rice is al dente, continue cooking with hot water as the liquid.

6. As soon as rice is al dente, remove pot from the heat. Season with salt if needed and serve in bowls.

Note

Homemade broth is far superior to store-bought in this recipe.

Stuffed Peppers
In memory of my mother

2 cloves garlic, chopped
1 cup breadcrumbs
1 egg
10 small capers
2 green bell peppers
1/4 cup olive oil
tomato sauce

1. Preheat oven to between 350 and 400 degrees F.
2. In a large bowl, combine garlic, breadcrumbs, egg, and capers. Mix well until filling comes together. Set aside.
3. Blanch peppers in boiling water for about 3 minutes. Remove and let drain for a few minutes.
4. Cut tops off peppers and use stuffing to fill. When peppers are full to the top, place in a deep pot and drizzle with olive oil.
5. Arrange peppers on a baking sheet and pour tomato sauce over. Bake uncovered until peppers are soft, at least 1 hour.

Note

The secret to making good stuffed peppers is to get that pepper soft. This is why I blanch the peppers for 10 minutes. My mother always made stuffed peppers for me and my two sisters.

Peppers and Eggs
In memory of my father

3 teaspoons extra-virgin olive oil

pinch of red pepper flakes

pinch of salt

1 onion

6 Italian frying peppers, cleaned, cored, and cut into long slices

2 eggs, scrambled

1 loaf Italian bread

1. In a frying pan, heat oil with red pepper flakes, salt, and onion.
2. Add peppers. Cover pan and cook until peppers are soft.
3. Pour eggs over peppers and cook until eggs are no longer running.
4. Remove peppers and eggs from the frying pan and place in half of the Italian bread.

Fried Mozzarella Sandwich

★ *Francis DiCandio*

3 eggs
pinch salt
2 tablespoons milk
5 slices stale bread
5 slices mozzarella cheese
all-purpose flour
oil for deep frying

Breads and Rolls

Garlic Bread

3 tablespoons extra-virgin olive oil, plus more for drizzling
pinch oregano
pinch salt and black pepper
3 cloves garlic
1 loaf Italian bread, cut on the diagonal into 1/2-inch-thick
   pieces

1. Preheat oven to 200 degrees F.
2. In a small bowl, combine olive oil, oregano, salt, pepper,
   and garlic.
3. Spread mixture onto bread slices and place on a baking
   sheet. Drizzle a little more olive oil over before putting in
   the oven.
4. Cook until toasted, about 15 minutes.

Tomato and Basil Bruschetta

Bruschetta (pronounced *brusketta*), a Roman staple, is probably as old as the city itself. The traditional version is nothing more than bread toasted (preferably over a fire) and drenched in fresh green extra-virgin olive oil. Delectable on its own, bruschetta has evolved into many forms. This is the classic version, and it is so very simple to prepare.

Serves 6

2 cups fresh ripe tomatoes, coarsely chopped
3 tablespoons fresh basil, chopped
1/2 cup extra-virgin olive oil (buy the highest quality you can afford), divided
coarse salt
1 (16-to-18-inch) loaf Italian bread, sliced about 3/4 inch thick (20 to 24 slices)
2 cloves garlic

1. Preheat broiler or grill until very hot.
2. In a medium bowl, combine tomatoes, basil, and 2 tablespoons oil. Set aside.
3. Place bread slices under the broiler or on the grill. Toast on both sides until pale brown. (A little charring can add some flavor, but the bread should remain tender and moist inside.)

4. Remove bread from heat and let cool until you can handle it. Rub one side of each slice with garlic, then brush with remaining oil.
5. Top bread with tomato mixture (leaving the juice in the bowl) and serve immediately, before the bread gets soggy.

Desserts

Chocolate Truffles
Francis DiCandio

Serves 6-7

6 balls hard-frozen chocolate ice cream
6 maraschino cherries
6 ounces unsweetened chocolate, cut into shavings

1. With a baller, scoop out a small hole in each of the balls of ice cream. Place a maraschino cherry in each and replace the scooped-out ice cream.
2. Roll ice cream balls in the shaved chocolate, coating them well.
3. Freeze the prepared truffles, removing from the freezer about 30 minutes before serving.

Note

I always had a weakness for chocolate.

Rum Syrup

1 cup water
1/2 cup sugar
1/2 cup rum

---

1. In a saucepan over low heat, combine water and sugar. Cook until reduced to about 2/3 cup.
2. Remove pan from heat and let syrup cool.
3. Stir rum into syrup and use as needed.

Pears in Red Wine

Francis DiCandio

4 firm pears
3 cups red wine
1/4 cup orange juice
sugar
1 cinnamon stick
2-inch piece orange zest
7 ounces mascarpone cheese

1. Peel pears, being careful to keep them whole with stalks attached.
2. In a large pan, combine wine, orange juice, and sugar. Stir over heat until sugar is dissolved.
3. Add cinnamon stick and zest. Add pears and stir gently to coat.
4. Cover pan and simmer until pears are cooked, 20–25 minutes. Allow to cool in syrup, then remove pears, leaving liquid behind, and drain on paper towels.
5. Bring liquid to a boil and boil rapidly without lid until only 3/4 cup remains.
6. Serve pears with a little syrup and mascarpone.

Liquor-Spiked Espresso with Whipped Cream

Francis DiCandio

2 tablespoons heavy cream

2 teaspoons confectioners' sugar

1 1/2 ounces bittersweet chocolate

12 ounces hot espresso

1 1/2 ounces Kahlua

1. In a small bowl, whip cream and sugar to soft peaks. Set aside.
2. In a heatproof bowl set over a pan of simmering water, melt the chocolate, stirring until smooth.
3. Divide melted chocolate evenly among 6 coffee cups. Top with espresso, Kahlua, and whipped cream. Serve immediately.

Note

Italians love espresso. I wouldn't be surprised if my mother fill my baby bottle with it!

Neapolitan Honey Balls

Francis DiCandio

4 egg whites
1/2 cup sugar
3 1/4 cups flour
1/4 cup butter
cooking oil
1/4 cup honey
1/2 teaspoon grated orange peel
1/2 teaspoon vanilla extract
1/2 teaspoon anise liqueur
finely chopped glazed fruit or confetti sprinkles

1. In a large bowl, beat together egg whites and sugar. Work in flour, more or less than the indicated amount, to make a dough that is soft but workable.
2. Roll dough out into cylindrical pieces about the size of a pencil and cut the cylinders into 1-inch lengths. Roll the lengths between the palms of your hands into balls.
3. In a frying pan, heat oil until hot. Drop balls into oil and cook until nice and brown.

Note

This is another great Christmas tradition I remember.

Olive Oil Cake

There's no butter or shortening in this recipe, only a little of Italy's liquid gold. The olive oil makes this cake especially moist and tender, and it lends a savory hint to the lightly sweet flavor. Use a milder extra-virgin olive oil rather than one of the peppery ones, and don't substitute vegetable or other oils—the results will be inferior.

3/4 cup extra-virgin olive oil, plus more for greasing the pan
1 1/2 cups all-purpose flour
1 1/2 teaspoons baking powder
1 teaspoon salt
3 eggs
3/4 cup granulated sugar
1/3 cup freshly squeezed orange juice
zest of 1/2 medium orange
1/2 cup milk
confectioners' sugar, for dusting

1. Move oven rack to upper portion of the oven and preheat to 350 degrees F. Grease bottom and sides of a 9-inch regular or springform cake pan with olive oil.
2. In a small mixing bowl, combine flour, baking powder, and salt. Set aside.
3. In a large mixing bowl, beat eggs briefly and add sugar. Beat until foamy, about 30 seconds.
4. Add 3/4 cup olive oil, orange juice, and orange zest; combine thoroughly, then beat in milk.

5. Add flour mixture and continue beating until everything is well combined and batter is smooth.

6. Pour batter into prepared pan and bake until cake starts to pull away from sides of the pan and a knife inserted into the center comes out clean, about 45 minutes.

7. Place the cake on a rack to cool for 10 minutes, then invert onto a rack to cool completely. Dust with confectioners' sugar.

Ricotta Cheesecake

This cheesecake has the slightly grainy texture of ricotta and is lighter than conventional American cheesecakes. Top it with chocolate sauce for added flair.

2 tablespoons butter, softened

8 ounces biscotti, flavor of your choice

6 eggs

3/4 cup granulated sugar

1/4 teaspoon salt

2 (15-ounce) containers ricotta, drained, room temperature

8 ounces mascarpone cheese or cream cheese, room temperature

2 teaspoons vanilla extract

zest of 1 lemon

strawberries, raspberries, or blueberries (optional)

1. Set a rack in center of oven and preheat to 350 degrees F. Spread butter on bottom and sides of an 8-inch spring-form cake pan.
2. In a food processor, grind biscotti to a fine texture. Transfer to prepared pan and tilt pan around to coat the inside with crumbs. Tip out excess crumbs and discard.
3. In a large mixing bowl, use an electric mixer at high speed to whip together eggs, sugar, and salt for 2 minutes. Beat in ricotta, mascarpone, vanilla, and lemon zest.
4. Pour batter into crumb-lined pan and spread out with a spatula so the top is even and smooth. Bake until cake puffs up and turns light golden around the edges, about 1

hour 15 minutes. The center should still move when you shake the pan.

5. Set pan on a wire rack to cool completely; the center will sink slightly.

6. Serve with strawberries, raspberries, or blueberries, as desired.

Lemon Ricotta Cookies

Italian cookies tend to be drier and more crumbly than cookies made in the USA, but these are soft and moist. That's the ricotta at work.

2 1/4 cups all-purpose flour
1 teaspoon baking powder
1 teaspoon salt
1 stick (1/2 cup) unsalted butter, softened
1 cup sugar
2 eggs
1 (15-ounce) container ricotta cheese, drained
1/2 teaspoon vanilla extract
3 tablespoons lemon juice
zest of 1 lemon

1. Move oven racks to middle and top rungs, and preheat oven to 350 degrees F. Line two baking sheets with parchment paper or silicone baking mats.
2. In a medium mixing bowl, sift together flour, baking powder, and salt. Set aside.
3. In a large bowl, use an electric mixer on high speed to cream butter with sugar until light and fluffy, 2 to 3 minutes.
4. Switch to medium speed and add eggs one at a time, beating each until thoroughly combined with the butter. Add ricotta, vanilla, lemon juice, and lemon zest, and continue to beat to incorporate.

5. Reduce to low speed and add flour mixture. Beat just until the ingredients marry.

6. Scoop heaping tablespoons of dough onto prepared baking sheets, 2 inches apart. Bake, switching the pans halfway through the cooking time. The cookies should puff up and turn golden around the edges after 15–20 minutes. Remove from the oven and set the cookies in a single layer on wire racks to cool.

Note

This dough is great for any piecrust you wish to make.

Lemony Almond Macaroons

1 (14-ounce) package sweetened shredded coconut
1 cup sliced almonds
1/4 cup sugar
1 teaspoon grated lemon zest
1/4 teaspoon kosher salt
4 large egg whites

1. Heat oven to 325 degrees F. Line 2 baking sheets with parchment paper.
2. In a large bowl, combine coconut, almonds, sugar, lemon zest, and salt. Stir in egg whites.
3. Drop 2-tablespoon mounds of the mixture on the prepared baking sheets.
4. Bake, switching sheets halfway through, until edges of macaroons begin to brown, 20–25 minutes. Transfer to rack to cool completely.

Chocolate Banana Cream Pie

1 frozen pie shell, pricked with fork
1 package instant chocolate pudding, prepared
2 ripe bananas, thinly sliced
freshly whipped cream
1 dark chocolate bar, shaved with a vegetable peeler

1. Preheat oven to 425 degrees F.
2. Bake pie shell until golden, 10–12 minutes. Remove from oven and let cool.
3. Line pie shell with half the prepared chocolate pudding. Add a layer of bananas. Top with remaining pudding and banana slices. Cover with giant swirl of whipped cream, starting at the center and working out.
4. Top pie with chocolate shavings.

Note

This is my quick version of chocolate banana cream pie. It's not Italian, but it's good.

Maple Nut Coffee Ice Cream Dessert

2 pints coffee ice cream
1 cup salted mixed nuts, coarsely chopped
1/2 cup maple syrup, warmed

1. For each serving, place 2 scoops ice cream in a bowl and top with chopped salted mixed nuts. Drizzle with warm maple syrup.

This and That

Marinara Sauce

Makes 6 cups
2/3 cup olive oil
8 cloves garlic, sliced paper-thin
8 cups canned peeled plum tomatoes
1/2 teaspoon oregano
salt and pepper

1. In a saucepan, heat oil over high heat. Add garlic and cook until lightly browned.
2. Reduce heat to low and add tomatoes and oregano. (Take care—the tomato liquid may cause the fat to spatter.) Cover pan and let sauce cook 30 minutes or until it thickens. Crush tomatoes slightly during cooking, but don't mash; they should still be in recognizable pieces.
3. Season with salt and pepper to taste.

Note

Marinara sauce is a simple thirty-minute sauce to make.

Spring Sauce

Makes about 3 cups

4 scallions, finely chopped
1, finely chopped
1/3 cup finely chopped parsley
1/3 cup finely chopped sour dill pickle
2 cups mayonnaise
2 tablespoons white wine vinegar
salt

1. In a glass mixing bowl, combine all the ingredients, including salt to taste.
2. Let the sauce season in the refrigerator for 2 hours before serving with sautéed or fried fish.

Antipasto Dressing

Makes about 3/4 cup, enough for 4 servings of antipasto

1 teaspoon chopped parsley
1/4 teaspoon dried oregano, crushed
1/2 teaspoon salt
1/8 teaspoon white pepper
1/4 cup red wine vinegar
1/2 cup olive oil

1. In a mixing bowl, combine parsley, oregano, salt, pepper, and vinegar.
2. With a fork, beat olive oil into the mixture a little at a time. Correct the seasoning, adding more salt as needed.

Potato Dumplings

1 1/4 cups mashed cooked potatoes
1 cup flour
1 egg, beaten
2 tablespoons salt, divided
3 quarts simmering water

1. In a mixing bowl, smoothly combine potatoes, flour, egg, and 1/2 teaspoon salt.
2. Shape mixture into thick rolls about 1 inch long.
3. In a large saucepan, bring water to a boil. Season with remaining salt and add dumplings. Reduce heat and poach dumplings in simmering water for 5 minutes.
4. Drain dumplings well and serve hot with separate servings of sauce and freshly grated parmesan cheese.

Sweet Dough

Makes sufficient dough for bottom and top crusts for a deep-dish or 9-inch pie pan or for about 4 dozen small cookies.

2 1/4 cups flour
3/4 cup sugar
1/4 teaspoon salt
1 cup butter
1/4 teaspoon grated orange rind
2 egg yolks combined with 1/2 teaspoon vanilla extract

1. Sift flour, sugar, and salt together onto a pastry board or into a bowl.
2. Make a well in the center of the flour mound. In it, place the butter, orange rind, and egg yolk mixture. With your fingers, work those ingredients quickly into the flour mixture to produce a thick smooth paste.
3. Shape dough into a ball, wrap in waxed paper, and chill for 30 minutes. Use as required in specific recipes.

Potatoes, Family Style

6 large potatoes, peeled, washed, and cut into 9 or 10 odd-size
  pieces each
1/2 cup olive oil
2 large cloves garlic, peeled
3 sprigs Italian parsley, with stems
1 bay leaf
1/4 teaspoon rosemary
3 fresh sage leaves
salt and pepper

1. Dry the potato pieces thoroughly on paper toweling.
2. In a large skillet, heat oil. Add potatoes and sauté briskly,
   stirring constantly to brown evenly.
3. Add garlic, parsley, bay leaf, rosemary, sage, and salt and
   pepper to taste. Combine with potatoes.
4. Reduce heat to medium low and continue cooking
   potatoes, stirring occasionally, until tender, about 20
   minutes more.

Oil and Vinegar Dressing for Green Salad

Makes about 1/2 cup, enough for 6 servings of salad

1/4 teaspoon salt
1/8 teaspoon pepper
1 clove garlic, mashed
2 tablespoons wine vinegar
6 tablespoons olive oil

1. In the bowl in which the salad is to be served or in a small mixing bowl, combine salt, pepper, garlic, and vinegar.
2. Gradually add olive oil, beating in with a whisk until an emulsion is formed.
3. Remove garlic before combining dressing with the greens.

Italian Grilled-Cheese Sandwich

Makes 2 sandwiches

8 slices mozzarella cheese
4 slices whole wheat bread
6 basil leaves
3 eggs, beaten
1 cup flour
1 cup olive oil

1. Place 4 slices of mozzarella on each of two slices of bread.
2. On top of each mozzarella pile, place 3 leaves of basil. Top with remaining 2 slices of bread.
3. Place eggs in one bowl and flour in another. Dip each sandwich in the flour first and then the egg mixture.
4. In a frying pan, heat olive oil. Add sandwiches and fry until crisp, turning once.

Ricotta and Herb Spread

1 (15-ounce) container fresh ricotta (about 2 cups)
2 teaspoons flat-leaf parsley
1/4 teaspoon kosher salt
1/4 teaspoon black pepper
2 teaspoons extra-virgin olive oil
1 small baguette, sliced and toasted

1. Spoon ricotta into a serving bowl.
2. Sprinkle ricotta with parsley, salt, and pepper.
3. Drizzle with oil and serve with bread.

Note

When I was growing in Brooklyn, my father would sprinkle a little sugar on the ricotta cheese and eat it just like that. Try it!

I was born in Brooklyn and now live in the great Queens neighborhood of Glendale. I love Italian food—and everything Italian.

About the Author

I was born and raised in the heart of Williamsburg, Brooklyn, in 1952. I have such great memories growing up in Brooklyn. My two sisters, Roseann and Angela, would jump rope or play hopscotch, and I would play stickball, punch ball, and stoopball. I really miss those good old days and all the games we played. I wish I could stop the clock. Thank you, Mom and Dad, for giving me and my two sisters a loving childhood. God bless you. I will carry you in my heart until we meet again.

Printed in the United States
By Bookmasters